Ages 5-7

NC Level 1
Scottish Level A

Extra Help
in
Maths

Practical special needs support

Rose Griffiths

acknowledgements

The publisher would like to thank the
following organisations and individuals for
their help or permission to use copyright
material: IKEA and Early Learning Centre,
Ruth Lyons, Emily Gartside and Kelly-Anne
Glenn. In addition, the author and publisher
thank Cas Beckett for word-processing the
original manuscript.

For the National Numeracy Strategy
Framework for Teaching Mathematics
© Crown copyright. Reproduced under the
terms of HMSO Guidance Note 8.

For the National Curriculum for mathematics
© Crown copyright. Material is reproduced
with the permission of the Controller of HMSO
and the Queen's Printer for Scotland.

For the Scottish National Guidelines for
Mathematics 5–14 © Crown copyright.
Material is reproduced with the permission
of the Controller of HMSO and the Queen's
Printer for Scotland.

Every effort has been made to trace
the copyright holders and the publisher
apologises for any errors or omissions.

Text © Rose Griffiths 2004
© 2004 Scholastic Ltd

Designed using Adobe InDesign™

Published by Scholastic Ltd,
Villiers House,
Clarendon Avenue,
Leamington Spa,
Warwickshire CV32 5PR

Printed by Belmont Press, Northampton

 1 2 3 4 5 6 7 8 9 0   4 5 6 7 8 9 0 1 2 3

British Library Cataloguing-in-Publication Data
A catalogue record for this book is available from the British Library.

ISBN 0-439-97107-1
Visit our website at www.scholastic.co.uk

author
Rose Griffiths

editor
Jane Gartside

assistant editors
Nina Bruges
Jon Hill

photography
Martyn F Chillmaid

series designer
Heather C Sanneh

designer
Heather C Sanneh

illustrations
Teri Gower/Malcolm
Sherman

cover image
Digital Vision

contents

Using
this **book**

This book has been written primarily for teachers and classroom assistants working in mainstream schools, who are looking for ways of helping children in the lowest 20% of the attainment range. Parents will also find plenty of activities here that they can share and enjoy with their children, to give them extra help in maths.

Organisation

The ideas are especially for those children who need more examples and more practice than others, to understand and remember each new mathematical concept.

This book includes four different sections of information:
- general advice about ways of working (pages 5–9);
- background mathematical information about:
  Number (pages 10–11),
  Calculations (pages 32–33) and
  Measures, shape and space (pages 42–43);
- double-page spreads of notes, ideas and illustrations to support particular mathematical topics;
- summary of objectives (pages 62–64).

Topic spreads

Each spread includes:
- notes on teaching and learning for that specific topic, to help with setting clear objectives for the work;
- examples of activities that children have enjoyed and found useful. These are explained briefly so that you can tailor them for use in any teaching situation: for example, as the main activity for a group of children in a whole-class lesson, or for a pair of children to do, working with additional adult help.

Photocopiable sheets

Some activities are supported by photocopiable pages that can be found on pages 52–61. These can be photocopied for use in school or at home. Colour copies are especially attractive to children, but black and white copies will also work well.

Summary of objectives

The main teaching objectives for each topic are summarised on pages 62–64. Pages 62–63 provide the relevant information for England while page 64 covers the curriculum for Scotland.

Planning
for success

Learning mathematics is not always straightforward, and children do not always learn at a steady rate. However, even at the age of only five or six, some children's slower progress in maths may be a cause for concern.

Fortunately, there are many ways in which we can help low-attaining children understand, remember and use mathematics more successfully. Many of the principles involved are equally helpful with children at all levels of attainment.

Causes of low attainment

The causes of children's low attainment in maths are very varied. Sometimes, with young children, it is simply lack of experience. Sometimes difficulties stem from the same problems that make it hard for children to make a confident start to reading (and this might include specific learning difficulties, or more general problems with concentration, memory, or processing language). Some children's problems arise because they have been 'moved on' to new work before they sufficiently understood the previous underlying concepts; children who have changed school or missed school may have significant gaps in their knowledge. Some children

have physical or sensory difficulties. Whatever the cause of a child's slow progress, there is always something you can do to help.

© SODA

Make-believe play is an enjoyable way of helping children think about how mathematics is used in real life

© CREATAS

Working with a partner is helpful in building confidence as they practise skills together

How to help

What are the best ways of helping children succeed? Here are some general principles to think about.

• **Show that maths is useful and enjoyable**

Maths *must* make sense to children. We need to make the most of children's own interests and experience at home and in school, to show them where and how maths is used. High motivation to learn is particularly important for those who find learning difficult, so enjoyment and a clear purpose are doubly important for low-attaining children.

• **Build confidence**

Unfortunately, sometimes children's previous experience of learning maths has been so unsuccessful that they lack the confidence needed to make good progress. The fear of getting things wrong can make some children feel so anxious that they put all their energies into avoiding work, using tactics ranging from spending a long time sharpening their pencils, to being naughty.

How can you give children fresh hope that it might be worth trying again? It can be helpful to tell

children that some parts of maths can be quite hard to explain, so it is not surprising that people don't always understand them first time. It is also worth emphasising that mistakes in maths can be very useful because they help point out something new you can learn. This is much better than *accidentally* getting something right, because then you don't find out that you didn't really understand it.

Working with a partner is useful in lots of ways, but can especially help build confidence as children practise explaining things to each other, comparing answers, and making up questions for each other.

When children are particularly stuck on one aspect of maths, it will often be more effective to switch to a different area of work for a while – ideally, one where success is guaranteed! Returning to a difficult idea after a breathing space is more helpful than a long stretch of failure.

• **Encourage children to be independent**

Children whose attainment in maths is low will often benefit from additional adult support. However, it is crucial to achieve an effective balance – providing the level of support children need to help them learn quickly and confidently, without giving so much help that they really haven't done any work themselves. Progress is not about leading children through a series of steps to the right answer; it is about helping them to the point where they are able to think for themselves about how they are going to solve a problem.

Discuss the pace of learning with children. Explain that you want them to learn as much as they can, so you don't want to go too slowly; but that you also don't want to go so fast that they haven't got

© CREATAS

time to understand new ideas. Encourage children to ask questions, to think about things they could do that would help them learn more, and to take joint responsibility with you for making the most of their time. Children can often help set short-term tasks or targets for themselves. For example: *'I'll practise counting backwards from ten every day this week'* or *'I'll learn how to spell two and four by Friday.'*

Use activities with a simple method of work, but which can be repeated with different equipment, or in a different order, or with other slight variations. Try to provide enough variety to hold children's interest, but without so many changes that you spend too much time explaining what to do.

Problems with reading can sometimes hold children back, compared to their peers. Two strategies are particularly useful:
• Look for ways of making the ability to read less necessary (by using aural and practical work, for example).
• Teach reading alongside maths (making the most of opportunities to use written maths material as non-fiction texts for reading, writing and spelling).

• Use varied teaching approaches

It is important to use a variety of teaching approaches to improve the chances of finding effective ways of working with each child. Variety can also help children concentrate for longer on a particular topic, and using two or three complementary ways of working to solve a problem can increase children's understanding of what they are doing. Within any individual teaching session, look for ways of using all the child's available senses, and encouraging them to be active learners.

A full repertoire of work in maths for children aged five to seven is likely to include practical work, role play, discussion and demonstration, using games and number equipment, mental methods, stories and songs. It is also likely to include using resources such as calculators, computers, videos, audio tapes and books. Sometimes children will work on their own; more often, they should work with a partner, in a group, or with the whole class.

© PHOTODISC, INC

Above: Even slight variations, such as using a different dice, can help children to concentrate longer on a single topic

Left: Work on shape and space is often accessible to all levels of attainment

Some children will have more significant difficulties and will have an Individual Education Plan (IEP) that results in their working towards the same objective for many lessons. In such cases, teaching variety is critical to maintaining the child's motivation and increasing the chances of finding a key to his or her understanding.

• Link assessment and teaching

Every child learns best when their teacher has clear objectives for teaching and learning. You need to match your objectives to what the child already knows and understands, and you need to have realistic but high expectations of how to build on that. However, it is not easy to find out what someone already knows and understands in maths, especially with pupils who are convinced they can't do anything!

Often, the best way of assessing a child's understanding is to give them a problem to solve or an activity to do, and to watch them and discuss their work with them. Whatever form of assessment you use, it is important to explain to the child what you want to achieve: '*I want to find out how much you already know about this so that we can decide what you need to do next.*' With low-attaining children, assessment needs to be done very thoughtfully, so that they are convinced it is helpful, not humiliating.

Children whose progress is slow or erratic do need reassurance that they really are making progress. You may want to consider repeating an assessment activity after a gap of a few weeks, to show children that they can do more now than they could a little while ago.

• Make the most of every possible opportunity to learn

Maths learning does not happen exclusively in maths lessons, of course, and children who need extra time

to think about new ideas, or to practise skills, can gain from making the most of mathematical elements right across the curriculum, throughout the school day, and at home. Quite small things can prove significant – the chance to play a game again with a parent or carer at home, or a display in the corridor where a child queues up to go in for lunch. Never underestimate the power of incidental learning!

How many turtles?

It can also be very valuable to look for ways of providing additional short 'teaching slots'. Allow five or ten minutes outside the usual time allocated for maths, when children can work with a partner or an adult on an activity already tried in a main lesson, or do some preparatory work to increase their chances of participating well in the next whole-class lesson.

• Use sensible strategies for differentiation

Differentiation is used to make sure that children at different levels of attainment all have access to work pitched at a suitable level: not so easy that it is boring, nor so challenging that it is impossible.

Children aged five to seven change extremely fast, and learn at very different rates, partly depending on previous experience. It is important to avoid putting artificial limits on their learning, either through the tasks you give them or through the way you organise your class into groups. If children are put into attainment groups, it is important to review those groups frequently, and to use them flexibly.

Use open-ended tasks as often as possible – those where children all work on the same investigation or activity, but at their own level, with resulting work at their own level of achievement. This is known as 'differentiation by outcome'.

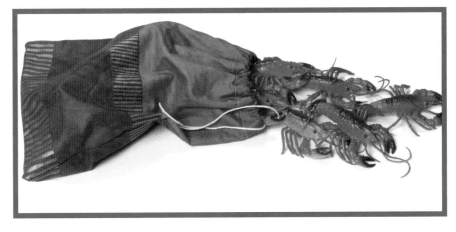

Work on shape and space (and sometimes measures) is often more accessible to children of all levels of attainment. Number, however, is more hierarchical, so there is more need to consider 'differentiation by task'. This involves providing separate activities for children at different levels of attainment (and sometimes a choice of equipment to use, to help children tackle an activity that would otherwise be too difficult).

You can sometimes differentiate by providing additional adult support. This will always be more effective if the adult knows not just what activity to do with the child or group of children, but what it is hoped the children will learn.

In whole-class lessons, some children may need particular kinds of help for introductory and plenary sessions, where children from the whole range of attainment are participating. Sitting close to the teacher, in a position where they do not have to talk across the entire class to answer the teacher's questions, can help children feel more comfortable. A few minutes spent discussing 'what we are going to learn in our next lesson' shortly before the lesson can improve children's confidence and concentration (in much the same way that reading the 'blurb' on the back of a book helps adults engage with a novel). Children may contribute to a plenary session more successfully if they are able to rehearse what they would say or show with another child or small group during the main part of the lesson.

© PHOTODISC, INC

If children are put into attainment groups, it is important to review those groups frequently, and to use them flexibly

Extra Help in **Maths**
Ages 5–7 NC Level 1 Scottish Level A

Extra help
with **number**

Children's work with number starts long before they start school, as numbers are such a prominent feature of our everyday lives.

Counting

It takes a surprisingly long time for children to learn to count accurately. For many low-attaining children, arithmetic starts to go wrong when they are asked to work with numbers that are bigggger than the largest number they can count accurately.

Regular counting practice is often the first and most important step in helping a low-attaining pupil to advance and improve.

© SODA

It is very important that children continue to have the opportunity to practise counting, using larger and larger numbers as they gain in confidence, right to the end of primary school. Counting is the basis of all arithmetic. Children who have a strong 'feel' for the size of numbers and who understand how our number system uses counting in ones, tens, hundreds and so on, will be more confident and capable when they add, subtract, multiply and divide.

At the earliest stages, what does learning to count involve? When you watch children counting a small group of objects, look for four important aspects. The first three can be learned alongside each other, and can happen in any order. They are all aspects of counting that adults can point out to children to improve their skill:

Knowing the number names (one, two, three…) is not just learning the words, but learning the correct order and being able to say them forwards or backwards. **One-to-one correspondence** is where we count one number to each thing we are counting, without missing any out, and without

© CLARA VON AICH/SODA

counting anything twice. Cardinality can be a difficult aspect to spot; it means that the answer to a 'How many?' question is the last number we count, not the whole string of numbers. For example, it is 'Four', not 'One, two, three, four'.

The fourth aspect of counting is one that develops gradually, as children's counting becomes more accurate:

Conservation (or invariance) of number is the term used to describe the fact that the number of objects in a group does not change, as long as none is added or taken away. To an adult this may seem obvious, but children often have doubts. Imagine you are not very good at counting. The first time you count a group of teddies, you make it five; but the next time, there seem to be six. It isn't unreasonable for the child to think that the number can change. See pages 12–27 for further information and activities.

Reading and writing numbers

Recognising or reading numbers precedes the ability to write them. Children do not learn to recognise numbers in order. Instead, they begin quite reasonably by learning the ones that have most significance for them, such as their ages. It helps to link counting practice with number recognition, such as finding the correct number from a set of numerals or number cards. Alternatively, give children a number card to read to tell them how many things you want them to count.

Children need to be able to recognise numbers written or printed in all sorts of different ways, but they only need to learn to write them in one way. If your school has a handwriting policy, check whether it includes advice about writing numbers. See pages 28–31 for further information and activities on reading and writing numbers.

Addition and subtraction

The ability to count a particular number of objects accurately (and to have done so often enough to be convinced that the number does stay the same) gives a solid foundation to number work within that total. For example, as soon as a child is consistently able to count a group of six objects accurately, you can begin to do practical problems using addition and subtraction in everyday contexts within a total of six. See pages 32–41 for further information and activities on addition and subtraction.

Songs and rhymes

In order to count efficiently, children need to know number names in order, and number songs and rhymes are one of the most enjoyable ways of achieving this.

Using rhymes reinforces the order of numbers and helps to establish the 'one more' or 'one less' relationship of each number to its neighbour.

Use a mix of familiar and new songs and rhymes. The familiar ones build confidence. The new ones require children to listen, to concentrate and to memorise: these are all useful skills for mathematics, too. Outside the classroom, you can assist parents and carers to help children learn a new song by providing them with the words and the tune.

Most rhymes involve counting quite small numbers (often only up to five or ten). Adapting songs and rhymes gives children the chance to extend counting to larger numbers if they wish. It also gives you the opportunity to provide different contexts in songs about counting, without having to learn new tunes.

© PHOTODISC, INC

It is often helpful to talk through the 'story' of a song in everyday language, asking questions to make sure the child understands what it is about. For example, introduce the song 'Five little speckled frogs' like this: *We're going to sing a counting song about some frogs. They were all sitting on a log next to a pond, looking for things to eat. Do you know what frogs like to eat?* Children can then focus their attention on the process of counting in the song.

- Help children keep track of the numbers in songs or rhymes by using fingers, props or number cards.

- Children need to hear a song very frequently when they are learning it. Give children a tape of the song to listen to at home or at school. You can record the children in your class (or in an older class) singing, to make your own tapes. If possible, give less confident children some practice with a new song shortly before singing it with the whole class.

- Make song sheets for children to illustrate and take home. See photocopiable page 52 as an example.

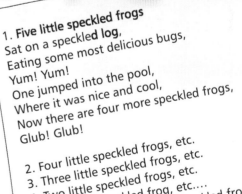

1. **Five little speckled frogs**
Sat on a speckled **log**,
Eating some most delicious bugs,
Yum! Yum!
One jumped into the pool,
Where it was nice and cool,
Now there are four more speckled frogs,
Glub! Glub!

2. Four little speckled frogs, etc.
3. Three little speckled frogs, etc.
4. Two little speckled frogs, etc.
5. One little speckled frog, etc....
… Now there are no more speckled frogs,
Glub! Glub!

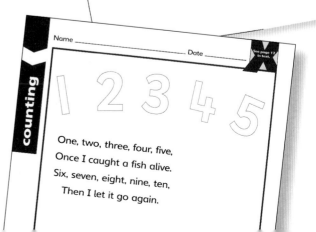

Name _____

Date _____

counting

1 2 3 4 5

One, two, three, four, five,
Once I caught a fish alive.
Six, seven, eight, nine, ten,
Then I let it go again.

Adapt familiar songs and rhymes.

Counting forwards

Peter hammers with one hammer,
One hammer, one hammer,
Peter hammers with one hammer,
All day long.

Introduce actions to emphasise the counting: make a fist with one hand, and thump on your thigh in time to the music:

Peter hammers with two hammers
(thump with two fists);

Peter hammers with three hammers
(thump with two fists and stamp one foot as well);

Peter hammers with four hammers
(thump both fists, and stamp both feet).

Use children's own names to personalise this song:

Katie hammers with one hammer…

One potato, two potato, three potato, four,
Five potato, six potato, seven potato more.

Some children want to know why it isn't two potatoes in this rhyme; it just isn't!

Think of other words to fit this rhyme:

One tomato, two tomato, …

One banana, two banana, …

One samosa, two samosa, …

One pot noodle, two pot noodle, …

One piranha, two piranha, …

Counting backwards

There were ten in the bed,
And the little one said, 'Roll over, roll over.'
So they all rolled over and one fell out.
There were nine in the bed …

Start at any number you choose; change the number who fall out if you want to:

There were eight in the bed,
And the little one said, 'Roll over, roll over.'
So they all rolled over and two fell out.
There were six in the bed…

Ten green bottles, hanging on the wall.
Ten green bottles, hanging on the wall.
And if one green bottle should accidentally fall
There'd be nine green bottles, hanging on the wall…

Make up variations of your own:

Five red dragons, sitting on a wall…

Seven pink parrots, perching on a wall…

Five currant buns in a baker's shop,
Big and round with a cherry on the top.
Along came Kayleigh with a penny one day,
Bought a currant bun and took it away.

Change the child's name, and buy two buns sometimes:

Along came Joe with two pennies one day,
Bought two currant buns and took them away.

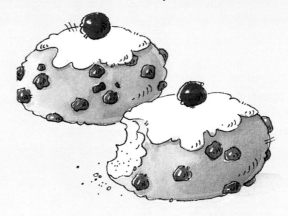

Counting books and stories

While children are learning to count, counting books and stories provide a lively and engaging way to assist in number recognition and ordering.

There are vast numbers of books available that vary greatly in their quality and interest level. If you have several counting books available, spend time with your children reading them and talking about them, to find out which ones the children find most interesting and appealing. Two of my favourites are: *Ten, Nine, Eight* by Molly Bang (published by Red Fox) and *Cockatoos* by Quentin Blake (also Red Fox). Children can also make counting books based on their own ideas and interests, using any numbers in any order.

Many story books include opportunities to count elements in the illustrations. However, counting things in a picture can be very challenging as it is difficult to keep track of which items have already been counted, when they cannot be moved out of the way. It is important to discuss this with children, so that they realise the importance of counting each item only once.

Stories do not have to be in books, of course. Oral stories with a simple structure can provide another engaging way of focusing children's attention on the importance of counting, comparing, adding and taking away. You can use props, puppets and the children themselves to help bring a story to life. Asking children to retell a story (or part of the story) will help consolidate their work.

● Use toy snakes, some leaves, silver foil (to represent water) and a cardboard box (as the cave) to tell this story:

Once there were five snakes slithering along the ground…
One, two, three, four, five.

First they went under the leaves…
One, two, three, four, five.

Then they went through the water…
One, two, three, four, five.

Then they slid into the cave…
One, two, three, four, five… GONE!

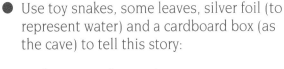

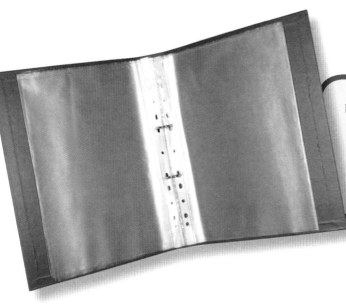

Make a counting book

Use an A4 ring binder, with plastic pockets to put pages in, or a sheet of card for each page.

Add more pages using larger numbers as a child gains in confidence.

Make a book of numbers in order

Act as a scribe for the children when needed. Children can draw directly on to each page, or cut out drawings and stick them on the pages.

Count backwards as well as forwards

Children can use rubber stamps to print pictures, or use self-adhesive stickers.

Use a small rectangle of card to hide the answer on each page: lift-the-flap books are very popular.

Concentrate on two adjacent numbers

Use felt, shiny paper, wool and other materials to provide different textures to feel as you count each picture.

Make a book illustrated with photos

You could use digital photos pasted into a word-processing or desktop publishing program.

Change the order of the pages in your counting books sometimes, so the children don't learn by rote.

counting

Collections

Children need to practise counting, but will need motivating to concentrate and spend time improving their accuracy if they find this skill difficult to acquire.

They are more likely to try to count accurately when they are using items that they find attractive, because they will want to know how many there are. Obviously, different children like different things, so each child should be able to choose from a variety of items for counting, organised in a way that makes them easy to fetch, and easy to put away again. It also encourages children to concentrate for longer if they can repeat an activity using different equipment, with a new context.

Do not just have collections where everything looks the same. Collections with readily distinguishable items can help to develop children's appreciation of the conservation of number more quickly. In other words, if a child counts a collection twice and gets a different answer each time, he or she can more easily see that the collection has remained the same and therefore the counting must be wrong.

Craft activities, where children make a small collection of items, are very useful because you can keep asking each child: *How many have you made now?* It also helps the child because they are counting at a slower pace; for example, after they have made three items, they have plenty of time to look at the three while they are making number four. It helps them appreciate the size of each number, and the effect of adding one.

Toy shops, market stalls and department stores are often a better source of counting equipment than educational suppliers.

TOYS © IKEA

● Keep at least one collection at a time on display if you can. Store other sorted items in small carrier bags, in open baskets, or in plastic bowls, mugs or tubs. Each collection should look as inviting as possible!

Cars

Bottle top.

● Provide a piece of felt or coloured paper as a background for children to count a collection.

● Use salt dough or other modelling material to make little animals to count.

● See the photocopiable sheet on page 53 for a salt dough recipe and instructions for making the model animals.

Extra Help in **Maths**
Ages 5–7 NC Level 1 Scottish Level A

17

Counting games

To sustain children's interest and concentration when learning to count, practice sessions need to be frequent and varied. Counting games and activities offer a variety of contexts that children enjoy working with.

It is best if the games are co-operative rather than competitive, because it is then easier to encourage pairs of children to help each other. Checking provides each child with extra counting practice, but in a different role. They can also take responsibility for deciding which numbers to practise counting – often the children are more ambitious than you anticipate.

Particularly when children are still practising counting numbers of objects below ten, it is very important to check their accuracy as often as possible. Watching a child while he or she counts a small group of objects gives you the opportunity to see any problems that arise, and to emphasise things that will help. For example, stress that children should move objects out of the way once they have counted them, to avoid missing any out or counting any twice. Watch out for children who are still uncertain of the number order: *One, two, three, five, six, …*

> We each have some lorries.

> We're playing 'Boxes on lorries'.

> We decide on a number to practise, and we put that number of boxes on each of our lorries.

- To choose a number, children can throw a dice, or take a card from a small set of number cards, or just agree a number between themselves.

- When they have finished counting boxes on their own lorries, each child checks their partner's lorries. (This means each child has counted the practice number eight times).

- Put the boxes back and choose a new number to practise.

Each game shown here can be used in the same way, so you can provide variety without having to give new explanations of what to do. Each game uses eight 'boards' and up to about 80 'counters'.

Boxes on lorries

Copy the lorry on page 54 on to card to make eight lorry cards (about A5 size).

Use small blocks or cubes of Multilink to be 'boxes' to go on the children's lorries.

Elephants

Copy the elephant on page 55 on to card to make eight elephant cards (about A5 size). Use buttons, large sequins or pasta shapes to be 'jewels' to go on the elephants' blankets.

Food on plates

Buy or collect eight plain plastic plates. Make 'jam tarts' from salt dough (see page 53) and bake them. Paint the 'jam' with acrylic paint. Alternatively, make samosas, or fried eggs!

Shells on the beach

Cut out eight rectangles of yellow felt as 'sand'. Collect shells of different sizes to count.

Further ideas for using counting games can be found on pages 34 and 35.

Extra Help in **Maths**
Ages 5–7 NC Level 1 Scottish Level A

Bags and boxes

Once children can count at least three or four items confidently, work can start on the idea of estimating.

Children sometimes find this puzzling because, in their minds, it would be easier for them just to count. The children can grasp the concept better if you talk to them about why you are estimating instead of counting. Explain that, in real life, estimates are often used when there isn't time to count accurately, or when it is difficult to do so (for example, if the items to be counted are in a sealed packet).

It is important to stress that estimating is not just guessing, but should be based on previous experience of counting accurately. For example, if a child has often counted out six toy cars, then he or she should be able to look at another small pile of cars and say whether they think there are more or less than six: *I think there are about eight.*

With an adult

- Use a small drawstring bag. Put up to ten similar unbreakable items in it.

- Show a group of children the bag.

- Ask one or two of the children to feel the bag (they must not open it!), and say *what* they think is in there, and *how many* they think there are.

- Ask one of the children to open the bag and count out the items, to see how close they were.

So your estimate is six things…

…and I think they are animals.

Six was a good estimate.

With a partner

- Ask one child to shut their eyes and wait. The other child prepares the counting bag by deciding how many things to put in it, and how many to hide away.

- After the estimate is given, he or she can open the bag and count, to check. If appropriate, as an extension, the child can then work out how many things must be hidden away.

Open your eyes. Feel the bag. How many lobsters do you think there are?

My estimate is...

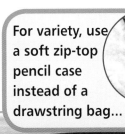

For variety, use a soft zip-top pencil case instead of a drawstring bag...

...or use a box you can't see into. Put up to ten unbreakable items in it. Instead of feeling the things to estimate, children can hold the box and listen carefully as they shake it gently.

Sounds and actions

Counting sounds and actions is quite different to counting objects, and can require a much higher level of concentration.

If a child's attention is diverted when she is counting a small group of objects, she can always start again. But if she is counting how many hops her friend does, or how many times you bang on a drum, she must not lose concentration midway.

Talk to the children about how difficult it is to count sounds or actions if they happen very quickly, or if several happen at once. Explain that the sounds or actions need to be one at a time, and not too fast, so they can be counted accurately. Children need practice at both counting sounds or actions made by someone else, and at making a particular number of sounds or actions themselves.

Counting actions out loud (for example, how many times a puppet nods its head) helps children focus on the number names in order. If a child is regularly having difficulty remembering a particular number name, you can help by making the puppet pause just before, say, the fifth nod and ask: *What comes next?* It can also help if the children keep a tally on their fingers as sounds or actions happen, to check against when they have finished counting out loud.

> For all of these activities, start quite slowly; when children are confident, go faster and use larger numbers.

Puppet counting

Use a glove puppet or a finger puppet to work with a group of children. Make the puppet sway from side to side, or bow low, or any other action that is easy to see, and ask the children to: *Count how many times the puppet bows.*

Counting actions

Counting can be an integral part of PE (and also at playtime and dinnertime, especially if you can enlist the help of a dinnertime supervisor). Choose an action and a number: *Can you hop five times?* Other suggestions could be to take big steps or to jump, stamp feet, clap hands or swing arms. Children could be encouraged to count when they are skipping, running, bouncing a ball, and so on. Check that children realise we do not usually say *one time* and *two times*; we say *once* and *twice*.

counting

Count my actions.
Then do the same!

clap, clap, clap!

Three!

Clap, clap, clap!

Copy me

Play this with the whole class or a group of children. Then they can play in twos or threes, taking it in turns to be the leader.

Other suggestions for copying could include them patting their heads, sticking out their tongues, waving their hands, standing up and sitting down or nodding their heads.

Noisy cards

Photocopy page 56 on to card to make four number cards, and four sound cards.

3 4 5 6

0 9 2 7

Play this game in pairs. One child chooses a number card and a sound card for their partner. The second child makes the chosen noise for the chosen number of times. Make more cards to vary the sounds or change the numbers.

Count the noises quiz

Make up a noisy quiz, which the children can rehearse to perform 'live' to the rest of their group or the class, or you can record on an audio tape to play back at a later date.

Quiz
1. 3 drum beats
2.
3.
4.
5.
6.

SCRIPT

Listen to our quiz.
There are six lots of noises.
Count each lot!

. . . .

Number one:
(3 drum beats)

. . . .

Number two:
(5 blows on a whistle)

. . . .

Track games

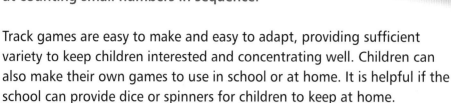

Track games provide very useful practice
at counting small numbers in sequence.

Track games are easy to make and easy to adapt, providing sufficient
variety to keep children interested and concentrating well. Children can
also make their own games to use in school or at home. It is helpful if the
school can provide dice or spinners for children to keep at home.

Initially, use plain, unnumbered tracks, so that the child concentrates on
moving their counter the right number of spaces, rather than thinking
about the number they will land on. Many children are unsure about
whether they should count the space they start on when they are
counting. They need reassuring that we count the hops. Demonstrate
frequently, and encourage children to help each other.

One aim in any counting practice is to help the child work accurately. In a
competitive game, a child's natural desire to win can overtake his desire
to be certain he has counted correctly! Working co-operatively can be
more effective for educational purposes. For example, have two children
working together to see which horse gets to the end of the track first.
Ensure each child takes it in turn to move both horses,
rather than giving the children one horse each so that
they compete against each other.

Which ghost will get to the end first?

- Start with a track drawn on a large sheet of paper.

- Use small toys, tops of shampoo bottles, or child-
  made tokens as counters.

- Change counters, to change the context.

- Change the dice, or use a spinner, to change the range of numbers to count.

counting

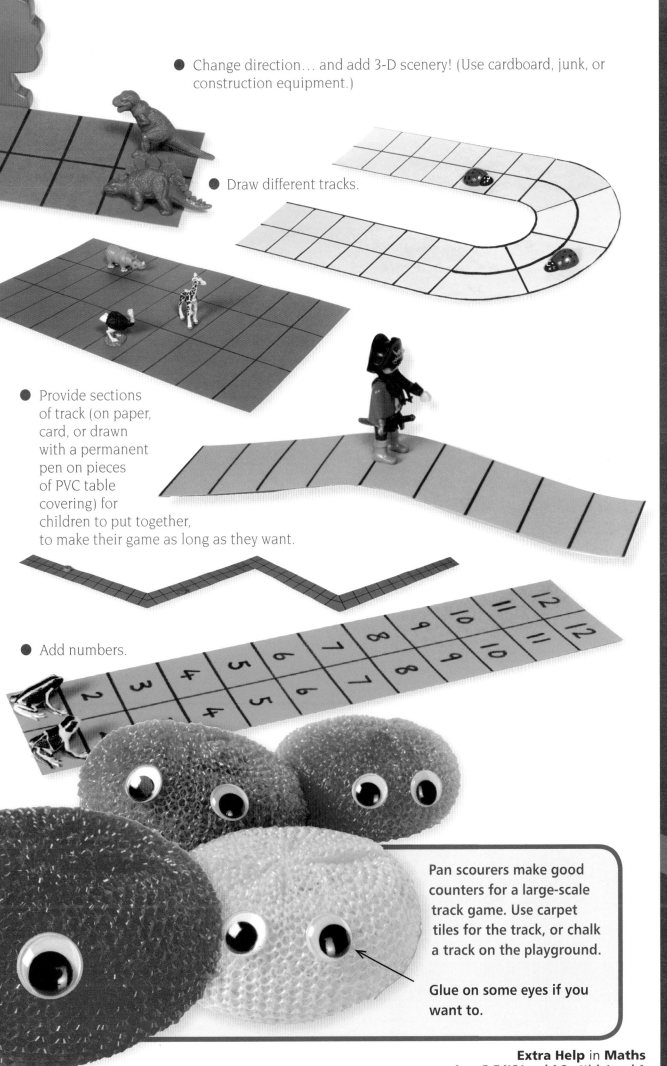

- Change direction… and add 3-D scenery! (Use cardboard, junk, or construction equipment.)

- Draw different tracks.

- Provide sections of track (on paper, card, or drawn with a permanent pen on pieces of PVC table covering) for children to put together, to make their game as long as they want.

- Add numbers.

Pan scourers make good counters for a large-scale track game. Use carpet tiles for the track, or chalk a track on the playground.

Glue on some eyes if you want to.

Extra Help in **Maths**
Ages 5–7 NC Level 1 Scottish Level A

Counting all around us

For children whose attainment is low, don't restrict counting purely to maths lessons – it is important to try and make the most of all the incidental opportunities that arise during the day.

Look for chances to 'model' counting, so that the children get to see and hear you counting for a purpose. Think about times during the day when children may be waiting for a few minutes (for example, queuing to go in for lunch) and see if it is possible to put something there for them to count while they are waiting.

Children who need extra help tend to improve their counting skills most quickly if they are given frequent, short periods of counting practice. It is worth trying to boost skills by providing not just daily practice, but by using five- or ten-minute sessions several times during the day. Encourage children to take responsibility for organising their own practice times (including practice at home), choosing a favourite activity to repeat and finding someone to check their counting when needed.

Everyday counting

Don't keep your own counting quiet! Say out loud what you are thinking: *There are six children on this table, so we need six pencils.* Similarly you can give children tasks that involve counting small numbers for you, such as: *Fetch me two sheets of paper, please. I need four children to carry these bats and balls! Can you please choose three story books for me?*

© SODA

© JAMES LEVIN/SODA

Role play and real life

Provide things to count in make-believe play areas. *How many tubs of margarine are there in the shop? How many letters have people brought to the post office? Can I have three bags of chips, please?* Ask children to count similar things at home, to link their role play with real life.

© STOCKBYTE

Make a poster

Before you start, decide where the poster will be displayed so that you make it a suitable size. Paint the background. For the example illustrated, the children used the photocopiable dinosaurs on page 57. Colour or paint the dinosaurs (or other things to count) and cut them out. If you want to, the dinosaurs can be fixed on with sticky tape or Blu-Tack, so that you can change the number every few days. Ask the children to count the dinosaurs as they are fixed on. Glue on a question (written by an adult, if needed).

Make a frieze

It is easier for children to count larger numbers if they can see the objects in a line. Use cut-outs (as with the dinosaurs above), or make multiple prints with a large rubber stamp. Friezes are useful along corridors.

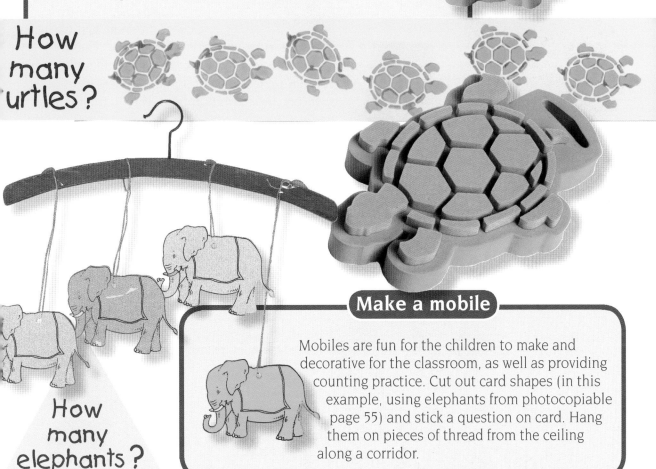

How many turtles?

How many elephants?

Make a mobile

Mobiles are fun for the children to make and decorative for the classroom, as well as providing counting practice. Cut out card shapes (in this example, using elephants from photocopiable page 55) and stick a question on card. Hang them on pieces of thread from the ceiling along a corridor.

Reading numbers

Children who are slow to get started on reading ordinary words may also take longer to recognise and remember numerals. Some children need reassuring that although numbers *can* be written using words (*one, two, three...*), we usually use a quicker way of writing numbers (*1, 2, 3...*).

The first number that most children recognise is probably their age, when they are 3 or 4 years old, particularly if they have had birthday cards with badges showing that number. They may also quickly learn to spot numbers that have special significance for them, such as the number of a bus route, or a door number. Numbers are written or printed in a variety of styles, and children gradually need to learn to read numbers in as many forms as possible (although they will only need to write numbers in one form).

It is helpful to link counting practice and number recognition from quite an early stage, but best to leave writing numbers until after children have had plenty of experience of reading them.

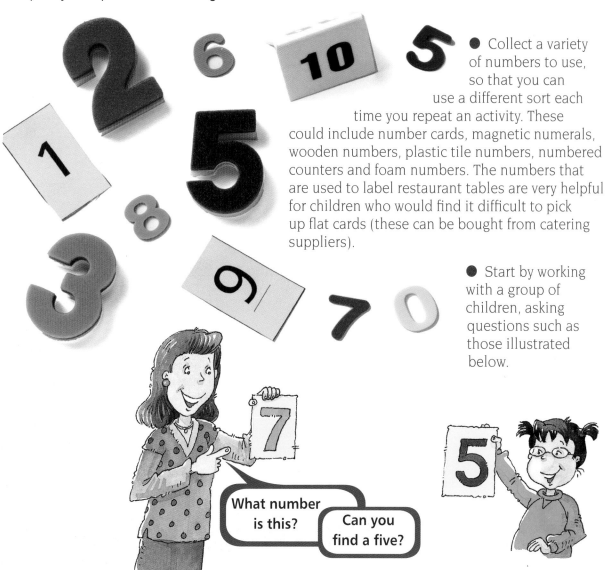

● Collect a variety of numbers to use, so that you can use a different sort each time you repeat an activity. These could include number cards, magnetic numerals, wooden numbers, plastic tile numbers, numbered counters and foam numbers. The numbers that are used to label restaurant tables are very helpful for children who would find it difficult to pick up flat cards (these can be bought from catering suppliers).

● Start by working with a group of children, asking questions such as those illustrated below.

What number is this?

Can you find a five?

© DIGITAL VISION LTD

Number running

Put a set of number cards at one end of the hall or playground, and a matching set at the other end. Choose one card and show it to a child. He or she has a good look, then runs to the other end to fetch a matching card. That child then chooses another card to show for the next child to run and fetch a matching one.

Number posts

Play this like the game 'North, south, east and west'. Choose four or five numbers that you want the children to practise reading. Write each one on a sheet of A4 paper, and fix these around the hall. When you shout a number, everyone has to run there.

Crayon rubbing

Make cut-out numbers from card. Show the children how to put one of the numbers under a thin piece of paper, and rub over it with a wax crayon. This activity helps them to concentrate on the overall shape of each number. Number outlines can be found on photocopiable page 58.

Counting on plates

Demonstrate these activities first and then let the children work in pairs. Each pair needs four paper plates, number cards 1 to 9, and up to 30 objects to count. One child lays out the plates and puts a number card on each one. Their partner then tries to put the correct number of objects on each plate. They should reverse roles after each turn. The activity itself can be reversed, with the first child placing up to nine objects on each plate. The partner then counts the objects and chooses a number card for each plate.

reading and writing numbers

Writing numbers

Learning to write numerals is very straightforward for some children, while others seem to have never-ending problems with reversals, unreadable numbers, and 5s that look like the letter 'S'.

Before you try to teach children to write numbers, they must be confident about recognising them. See pages 28 and 29 for further help with this.

The handwriting of numerals needs direct teaching and a reasonable level of enjoyable practice. The chart below is a reminder of the most common way of forming each number. It is important not to try to practise too many at once, and it can be helpful to concentrate on two or three numbers at a time that have something in common. For example, practise numbers two and three together, because with both of them you start at the top and go in a clockwise direction. See the box opposite for further suggested practice groupings. See also photocopiable page 59.

When they are still learning to write numbers, children need regular, individual, adult attention (a few seconds is often enough) to check they are forming their numerals correctly. Otherwise children will spend time practising how to write badly. Close attention at this early stage is essential, to avoid long-standing problems later on.

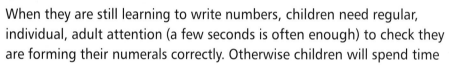

Explain that a 5 must have a straight line at the top, otherwise it might look like an 'S'. Children who are left-handed may use the methods shown, or they may prefer to form some numbers slightly differently.

Demonstrate

Before children write a numeral on paper, familiarise them with *how* to write it. One rule is helpful with every number: *Always start at the top!* On a blackboard, whiteboard, OHP or in the child's own book, show clearly how you write each number. Ask children to show you by 'going over' a number with their fingers, or drawing it in sand, on the palm of their hand, in the air, or on another child's back.

Practice

Group numbers together where they have a common feature to get the most out of practice sessions.

2 and 3 both start like this:

1 and 7 are straight.

4 and 5 are both written with two movements.

5 and 9 both have curved and straight bits.

6, 8 and 0 all start like this:

Variety

To maintain children's interest, vary the materials they use. Try chalk on sugar paper (or on slabs or tarmac). Squirt watery numbers on the playground using a washing-up liquid bottle. Use big felt pens, then medium ones, then thin ones and gradually reduce the size of numerals. Ask children to try pens and pencils of varying thickness, and to find the most comfortable writing position at their table.

© IMAGE 100 LTD

Good contexts

Provide as many purposeful opportunities as you can for involving children in writing numbers. Help them to make games or number cards; write today's date and the date of their birthday; collect car registration numbers; draw front doors and put numbers on them; make bus tickets or seat numbers for a make-believe play; draw their own number lines (see pages 36 and 37).

Minimise reversals

If children frequently write reversed numbers, there is a danger that they begin to see the back-to-front numbers as more familiar than the correct version. Discuss this problem with children, and say that if they are ever unsure about how to write a number, they should look for one to copy. They could look on a ruler, a number line, a clock, a calculator, a hundred square – or they could have a 'prompt card' of their own – to check. Correct any reversals; encourage children to check for themselves, too, after they have written a number.

Extra help
with **calculations**

Addition and subtraction should always be introduced to children in contexts that make sense to them, using numbers that they can count confidently and accurately. Early work on adding and taking away needs to be entirely practical, so that children understand what these problems involve, and can work out the answers with confidence, without being asked to put anything down on paper.

Practical approach

Use practical equipment including toys and other everyday items to make up problems like this: '*I had three books, then I got two more from my friend. How many books have I got altogether?*' At first, children will solve the problem by counting all the books; as they gain experience, they will no longer need to count '*1, 2, 3, 4, 5*', but will realise they can count on from three: '*3, 4, 5*'. Eventually, they will have done the sum 3 + 2 so many times that they know it by heart, and can give the answer without counting at all.

As well as toys and everyday items, you can work with more abstract materials such as counters or cubes, where children can use them to represent the items in their sum. Similarly, using your fingers to represent objects is useful.

Many children find that drawing a problem helps them understand what to do. Children's drawings of problems will often become more symbolic, as they realise they do not need detailed pictures to come to a conclusion. '*There were 2 cats in the garden, then 2 more came along. How many cats in the garden altogether?*' Emma's drawings of cats (right) became less detailed as she worked on this problem.

Gradually, children become able to imagine objects in their heads rather than always needing to see or handle them in order to carry out a calculation. This is an important step in developing mental calculation skills.

As mentioned above, children's recording of their work in addition and subtraction generally starts with drawing pictures to show what happened. Sometimes they will also use numbers to help

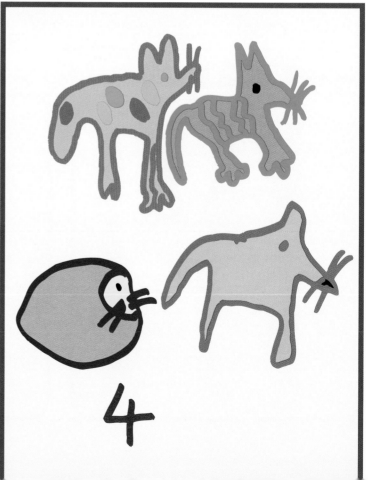

explain what they did. The next step will be to use numbers and the symbols +, = and –. Using a calculator can help to consolidate their successful use of these symbols, as they need to think carefully about which keys to press.

Develop mental skills

The number line is an important tool for practising counting, addition and subtraction. Imagining a number line in your head can also develop mental skills. However, the idea of a number line is quite

abstract, and low-attaining children may need extra time and practice to appreciate how to use one.

Counting practice continues to be important as children's skills in addition and subtraction grow. As their counting skills improve, you can introduce adding and taking away using bigger and bigger numbers – but always staying within the range that children can count accurately.

Familiarity with carrying out particular sums leads to children using more efficient strategies to carry out calculations, both practically and mentally, and they also begin to develop a repertoire of number facts that they know by heart. At this stage they will need to be given problems set in varied contexts so that they can practise using their skills.

What number am I hiding?

0   1   2   4   5   6   7

See pages 34 to 41 for further information and activities.

addition and subtraction

Practical problems

As soon as children are convinced about the conservation of number for a particular range of numbers, you can start work on practical addition and subtraction.

'Conservation' means that the number of items in a group will stay the same if you count them again, as long as none has been taken away or added to the group. This seems very obvious to an adult, but children need frequent experience of accurate counting to convince themselves. Until children believe this for a particular range of numbers, there is no point in moving them on to addition or subtraction. After all, if a child thinks a number can change when she or he just counts it again, they are not likely to think that two numbers added together will always give the same answer!

Addition and subtraction should always be introduced with an emphasis on practical, oral and mental work, using sensible and understandable contexts. Children will not always record their work at first; when they do, it may be by drawing a picture and just writing a single number as the answer to a problem, rather than writing a sum. More symbolic and abstract forms of recording follow later on.

Children's methods for adding will become more sophisticated as they gain in experience. At first, for example, they will add 2 and 3 by counting out 2, counting out 3, then counting all of them: *1, 2, 3, 4, 5.* Later, children realise that they can save time by counting on three from the first number: *3, 4, 5.* Further experience (including seeing what other people do) helps them see that it is quicker still to start with the bigger number and count on two: *4, 5.* Eventually, the child reaches the point where they have done the sum 2 + 3 so often that they have no need to count at all, because they know the answer by heart.

Adapting counting games

Many activities that have been used for counting practice can also be used for addition and subtraction. For example, the counting games on pages 18 and 19 provide useful contexts for problems.

Children can throw a dice twice to get the numbers for their sum, or take two cards from a set of number cards, or just choose their own numbers.

They use the practical equipment to find the total each time. Each counting game can be used in the same way.

We're adding jam tarts.

We each have a plate.

It's my turn to make up a problem. If you have 2 red jam tarts, and 3 orange ones, how many have you got altogether?

When children are responsible for making up their own sums, they will often be more ambitious than you expected. Children may also have ideas for further equipment to make or collect:

I had 9 marbles. I gave my friend 4. How many did I have left?

Using a calculator

Using a calculator alongside counting equipment is an excellent way of emphasising the symbols + and =, and, later on, − . If wished, use cards with the symbols and numbers to 'write' each sum.

© BIE BOSTROM/ SODA

I had 6 boxes on my lorry and I put on 2 more. How many boxes altogether?

Six add two equals...

● Both children try to work out the sum in their heads or with fingers.

● One child uses a lorry and boxes (see page 19).

● Their partner uses a calculator.

● When they have agreed on the correct answer, they write the sum down:

$$6 + 2 = 8$$

● For the next sum, they swap, and the first child has the calculator instead.

Increasingly, as they use equipment in different contexts, children will be able to 'picture' problems in their heads, and will not need to use equipment to get an answer: the beginnings of mental arithmetic!

addition and subtraction

Using the number line

The 'number line' gives us a very powerful mathematical image that many people find helpful when they are thinking about numbers or using mental methods of arithmetic. However, it is important to remember that it is a very abstract idea, and some low-attaining children are left baffled by things about it that seem obvious to others.

Children have often had experience of number tracks, before they are introduced to number lines. Number tracks (see pages 24 and 25) and number lines are different in two significant ways. Number tracks, such as those used for children's games, start with one, whereas number lines include zero. On a number track, we label the spaces, but on a number line, we label points on the line. This means that a number line is more adaptable, because later on we can, for example, put points in between the whole numbers and include fractions, or extend the line 'backwards' and include negative numbers.

Initial activities on a number line should concentrate on seeing numbers in order, and familiarising children with 'hopping' forwards and backwards, one step at a time. Then children can start to use the line for addition, using increasingly efficient strategies, and for subtraction. The more abstract nature of arithmetic on a number line also lends itself to practising a wider range of vocabulary for addition and subtraction.

> **All the activities described here are for work with a partner, but they all benefit from being introduced through work in a group.**

Cover-up

One child has two or three counters, to hide numbers on a number line. Their partner has to say what number is hidden. They take turns at this.

0   1   3   4   5   8

Make your own number line

Provide strips of card for each child, and a ready-made number line to look at. Resist the temptation to draw on a line and mark it for the child! Children can discuss what they need to do with their partner (including how long they want to make their lines).

Extra Help
Check handwriting if needed (see pages 30 and 31 for help).

One more, one less

One child chooses a number on the number line, and asks their partner a 'one more' or 'one less' question, such as: *What's one more than 5?*

They take turns at this, until they feel confident.

To help children develop a picture of the number line in their heads, try a harder activity: children have to shut their eyes when it is their turn to answer a question.

Extend the activity further by using a longer number line or 'two more' or 'two less' questions.

© PHOTODISC, INC

Adding

Adding on the number line will follow a similar pattern of development as adding with equipment, illustrated here with the sum 2 + 4.

First stage:

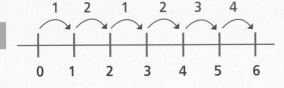

'Hop' each number in ones.

Second stage:

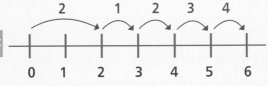

Go straight to the first number, then hop in ones.

Third stage:

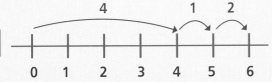

Start with the bigger number, then hop in ones.

When you are working with children directly, help them build a more varied vocabulary, by using two (or sometimes three) ways of phrasing questions during a particular session. *What's 2 add 4?* and *What's 2 plus 4?*, for example.
Do the same with examples for subtraction: *What's 4 take away 2? What's 4 minus 2?*

Count or hop

Use a 0 to 10 number line, ten objects to count, and two sets of 0 to 5 number cards (or 0 to 5 dice).

Shuffle the cards and take two of them. One child uses the number line, and the other uses the equipment, to get their answers. If they agree, they both write it down.

$3 + 1 = 4$

For the next sum, they swap, and the first child has the counting equipment.

addition and subtraction

Number facts

Once children have made a confident start to addition and subtraction through practical work with small groups of objects, you can start to work on two further ideas: number 'families', and missing number problems.

A number 'family' is the term sometimes given to a group of sums that have the same total. For example, the 'family' of 4 is 0 + 4, 1 + 3, 2 + 2, 3 + 1 and 4 + 0. Familiarity with these sums also helps children with subtraction, as they learn the linked facts: 4 – 0 = 4, 4 – 1 = 3, 4 – 2 = 2, 4 – 3 = 1, 4 – 4 = 0. This ability to separate (partition) a given number into two groups is very important. Investigating groups of linked sums like this helps children begin to see patterns in number relationships, and helps many children to start to learn an increasing repertoire of number facts by heart.

Missing number problems can be introduced as practical puzzles as soon as a child is confident about the conservation of number, within the range of numbers that they can count accurately. For example, if a child can count a group of six objects confidently, then you can do missing number problems using up to six objects. Show them five things, for example, then ask them to shut their eyes while you hide two. When they open their eyes, and can see three things, children have to figure out how many objects are missing. The methods children use to solve missing number problems are quite varied. They are not likely to use subtraction; it is much more common to use 'counting up', or trial and improvement (that is, making a guess, then adjusting it if it does not work). Of course, children may just know the answer, because they know the number fact '3 + 2 = 5' by heart.

Use any of these activities with whatever range of numbers children are confident about counting.

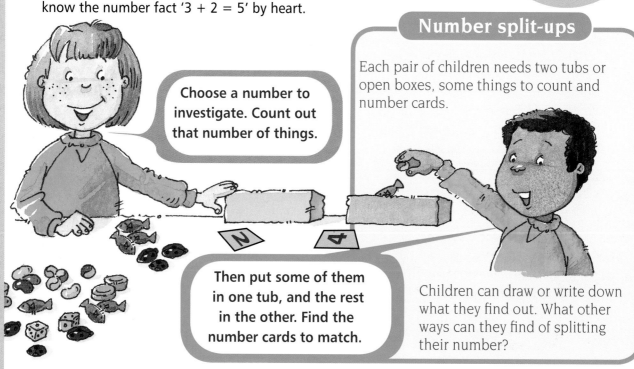

Choose a number to investigate. Count out that number of things.

Then put some of them in one tub, and the rest in the other. Find the number cards to match.

Number split-ups

Each pair of children needs two tubs or open boxes, some things to count and number cards.

Children can draw or write down what they find out. What other ways can they find of splitting their number?

Car park

Choose a number to investigate. Draw a 'car park' for toy cars, with that number of spaces. Children take it in turns to ask each other car park questions, like this:

There were 6 cars in the car park. How many spaces?

There were 3 spaces left in the car park. How many cars were already parked there?

Use toy cars to help make up the questions, and to answer them. Children can draw or write about some of their questions.

Roll-a-penny

Choose a number to investigate. Use that number of pennies. Draw a circular 'target' on a piece of paper.

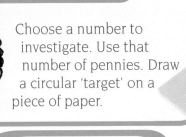

> I rolled 7 pennies. I got 3 on the target. I missed with 4!

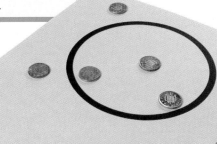

$$7 = 3 + 4$$

Tub puzzles

Each pair of children needs a plastic tub and some things to count. Choose a number to investigate.

> Count out that number of things. Show your partner...

5

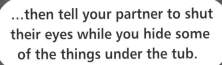

> ...then tell your partner to shut their eyes while you hide some of the things under the tub.

> Ask your partner, 'How many have I hidden?'

3

$$2 + \boxed{} = 5$$

addition and subtraction

Money

Money provides a very useful context for addition and subtraction, and is especially helpful for two particular aspects of subtraction: giving change by 'the shopkeeper's method' of counting up, and finding differences, for example between two prices.

To start with, check children's ability to recognise coins of different denominations. Some children learn to do this very quickly, but some need considerable practice. This work must be done with real coins; card and plastic coins are only useful once children are absolutely confident with real money! It is worth discussing the fact that there is no direct relationship between the size of a coin and its value – so, for example, a 5p coin is smaller than a 2p coin. Talk about the fact that the 'silver' coins are all worth more than the 'bronze' ones, and look at the £1 and £2 coins, too. Find the numbers on each coin that tell you how much each one is worth, and practise swapping each coin up to 20p for the right number of pennies.

You do not have to wait for a child to recognise all eight coins before starting on 'shopping' activities; just limit the coins you use to the ones you are concentrating on.

When you count up how much money you have in a handful of small change, you are, in effect, adding several small numbers together. Reading a price and finding the right coins is a similar problem. Adding two or more prices (using either just pence, or just pounds, but not a mixture) is another way of practising simple adding. Well-focussed role play is also very helpful, especially when it is linked with real-life experience with parents and carers.

THE ROYAL MINT

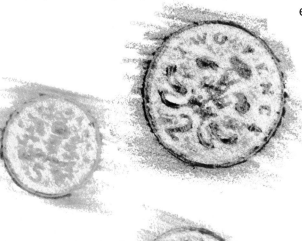

Coin rubbing helps draw children's attention to the size and shape of each coin, as well as the number on it.

Coin rubbing sums

Children work with a partner, using 1p, 2p and 5p coins. Each child 'rubs' up to five coins; their partner has to say what they add up to.

Count in twos

Use ten 2p coins (or more). Children give some to their partner. How quickly can the partner tell how much money they've got?

Secret coin challenge

A child hides a coin in a tissue – or in a baby's cotton sock! He or she asks their partner to say what it is without looking. If they struggle, they can practise with coins that are not hidden, then try again!

Find all the ways

Choose an amount of money from 4p to 10p. Children find all the ways they can to make that amount using different combinations of coins, and draw them (or use rubbings or coin rubber stamps). Try this for other amounts of money.

Toy shop

Set up a toy shop using small soft toys. Make all the prices £1, £2, £3 or £4. (Children may need to practise writing £ signs, before they write the price labels. Alternatively, use the labels provided on photocopiable page 60.) Give each customer a bag of 'pound coins' (either plastic coins, buttons or counters) to go shopping.

Set up other shops, according to children's interests, with prices in pounds or pence.

Price differences

Two or three children work together to make ten cards, showing prices from £1 to £10 and a picture of something you could buy for each price. (Use children's own drawings, or cut small pictures from a catalogue.) The children shuffle the cards, and take turns at taking two cards, then working out the difference in their prices. *The doll is £10, and the bus is £7, so that's a difference of £3.*

© IMAGE CLUB

Extra help
with **measures, shape** and **space**

Many topics in measures, shape and space are accessible to children across a wider range of attainment than with work in number, so it is easier to work with a whole class. You may also find that some children who struggle in number have a good 'feel' for shape and space, or vice versa: maths is a very varied subject, and people's attainment in different areas of maths can vary, too.

Maths is also a subject that has many links between the different areas within it. One result of this is that children's low attainment in number work can sometimes cause them difficulties in measures or shape and space. For example, a child who is not yet confident with recognising numbers 1 to 12 may be slow to get started on reading 'o'clock' times. This does not mean you have to wait until the child knows all the numbers before beginning to tell the time; often, children (and adults) learn faster when they can see a useful context and purpose to their learning. However, it is helpful to be aware of children's potential difficulties, and, in this example, it helps build children's confidence to start with the afternoon times, and concentrate on 1 o'clock, 2 o'clock, and so on.

© IMAGE CLUB

Measures

Which teddy is the smallest? Who has the biggest glass of squash? Who can jump the furthest? How long until tea time? Children are interested in measuring and comparing all sorts of things in their everyday lives, and gradually develop an increasingly sophisticated vocabulary to explain what they mean. As with other new words, children need to hear them being used in context, and to say and use them themselves. Bear in mind, though, that the words we use to describe the size or quantity of things are all used *comparatively*. For example, even a word as simple as 'big' depends for its meaning on

the context. Think of a big house, a big planet, a big butterfly… the 'big' is compared to other things of the same sort, so a big butterfly is actually very small compared to a house! This can be quite confusing for young children.

Learning about length, mass (weight) and capacity follows a similar pattern, looking at these important aspects of measuring:

Direct comparison. If we just need to know which is the smaller of two things, or whether they are the same size, often the simplest way of finding out is to compare them directly. If we want to know which skipping rope is the longer, we can lay them out next to each other (making sure they are aligned at one

Check that children are confident about which item is the heavier.

© DAVID MAGER/SODA

end) to compare. If we want to know which box of beads is the heavier, we could try lifting each box to see which *feels* heavier; or if the difference is not enough to judge by feel, then we can put them on each side of a balance. If we want to find out which of two empty shampoo bottles would hold the most, we can often tell by appearance; to check in case the appearance is misleading, we can fill the one we think is smaller, and see if the other one will hold all that plus more. Direct comparison of two items then leads to putting three or more in order of size.

Non-standard and standard units. Sometimes, direct comparison is not sufficient or convenient. Then we use either uniform non-standard units, or standard units, to measure. The non-standard units that most adults use when measuring length are convenient human ones: a hand span, or the length of your foot or a stride. In everyday life, we do not usually use non-standard units of other sorts (such as matchsticks or cubes). However, these can help children see how our standard system of measurement works, as you can, for example, move from counting matchsticks or cubes, to counting centimetre cubes, to seeing the link with a centimetre ruler (that is, using standard units).

See pages 44–47 for further information and activities on length and time.

Shape and space

Here are four ways in which you can help support low-attaining children's work in shape and space.

Support the learning of new vocabulary. Make sure children are hearing new words frequently and that they have frequent opportunities to use them themselves. Check for over- or under-generalisation of new words (for example, children using 'circle' to mean any curved shape, or restricting their use of 'square' to mean only those which are drawn parallel to the top and bottom of a page).

Improve observational skills. Use general activities where looking for similarities and differences is important, such as pairs games, dominoes and jigsaws. Find ways of helping children concentrate on detailed observation, through sketching, model making, and describing things.

Improve technical skills. Or find ways around shortcomings. For example, think about whether it is easy to use the drawing equipment you provide. A small bevel-edged plastic ruler is much easier for drawing lines than an 'infant' box-edged ruler.

Increase children's confidence. Provide peer support. Working with a partner is much less worrying than working on your own. Encourage children to watch what others do, and to copy each other's good examples. For example, many children's skill at using construction materials is enhanced enormously by spending time copying other children's models; they then become more confident about experimenting for themselves.

See pages 48–51 for further information and activities on shape.

Extra Help in **Maths**
Ages 5–7 NC Level 1 Scottish Level A

Length

As with other systems of measurement (such as measuring mass and capacity), children's work in measuring length will go through three broad stages.

Firstly, we concentrate on direct comparison of **two (and then more)** lengths, and develop the vocabulary children **need to talk about length.** This is more complicated than with some other **measurements, because** we use different words for length: for example, **long, longer, longest,** when we are comparing rivers or the length of people's hair; but tall, taller, tallest, when we are comparing people's heights.

Secondly, when children start to look at comparing lengths that cannot be directly compared (for example, the growth of a runner bean plant over a few weeks, or two items that cannot be moved next to each other), they can use non-standard units to measure. For example, you could measure the width of a chest of drawers with hand spans, then do the same to an alcove to see if it would fit. (The non-standard units do, of course, have to be of a uniform size for this to work. If someone with very large hands measured the furniture, and someone with very small hands measured the alcove, you might think it would fit when it would not!)

The third stage is to start using standard units: the measuring systems that people invented and agreed upon to make comparisons and record-keeping easier and more accurate. The metric system of standard units includes centimetres and metres.

Work on length is linked with work in number; for example, if you are using non-standard measurements you need to be able to count accurately. A centimetre ruler is obviously useful for measuring and drawing in centimetres, but it can also be used as a number line.

Snakes in a basket

Make snakes from strips of felt. Draw on eyes with a permanent pen, and glue on sequins or small felt shapes. Start with about five snakes, each of a different size, from about 7cm to about 14cm long.

● Count the snakes.

● Compare the snakes: take it in turns to choose a snake, then find a shorter one (or a longer one).

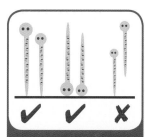

✔ ✔ ✗

Show children how to line up the snakes' noses or tails, to compare them.

- Can you put all the snakes in order of length?

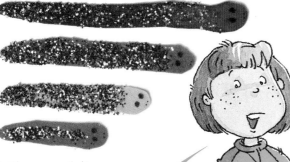

- Choose a felt snake. Can you make a paper snake, exactly the same length?

- Use a piece of A4 paper. Make the longest straight snake you can. Make the shortest, too!

- Make a set of paper snakes. Why do we need them to be straight snakes?

- Measure your snakes with cubes. Which snake is the longest?

This snake is just over 11 cubes long.

My smallest snake is 2 and a bit cubes long.

The difference in their lengths is about 9 cubes.

Show children how to put the cubes in a straight line, with no gaps in between them.

- Measure a snake with centimetre cubes, then use a centimetre ruler.

| 1 | 2 | 3 | 4 | 5 | 6 | 7 | 8 | 9 | 10 | 11 | 12 | 13 | 14 | 15 | 16 | 17 | 18 | 19 | 20 | 21 | 22 | 23 | 2 |

cm

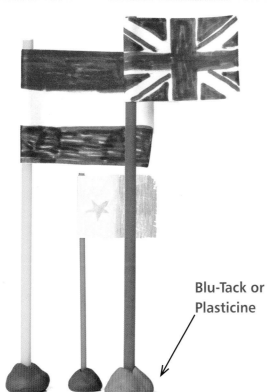

Blu-Tack or Plasticine

Flagpoles

Make flagpoles of different heights from drinking straws; tape on small flags made from card.

Compare them; put them in order; make more. Use the vocabulary of height: tall, taller, tallest; short, shorter, shortest.

Time

Time is a difficult system of measurement to work with, especially for young children. Some of their difficulties arise simply because they are young, so they have less experience of time passing than the adults around them. For example, children aged five have probably only just begun to notice the pattern of the seasons of the year; it is not until they have experienced it happening several more times that they will really appreciate what we are talking about when we refer to spring, summer, autumn and winter.

Time is a very abstract idea. You cannot see it or feel it, and the speed at which it passes seems to vary depending on what you are doing – so we talk about 'time going slowly' when we are bored, and the time 'whizzing past' when we are enjoying ourselves. To add to children's difficulties, the language of time can be quite confusing. Try explaining the words yesterday, today and tomorrow to a child who asks you 'Is it tomorrow yet?'

There are two aspects of work on time: order and duration. Children need to be able to put familiar events in order, according to what happens first, second, and so on. They also need to start thinking about how we measure amounts of time: how long is a minute, or an hour, or a day? And how do we keep track of time (using clocks and calendars, for example)? Children need to see where time is important in our everyday lives, to help them understand how we measure it.

© PHOTODISC, INC

What comes first?

Make sets of four or five cards, either by drawing pictures or taking photos, of a sequence of events. Use photocopiable page 61 to help you get started.

Shuffle the cards; can children put them in order again?

Once children have used one of these sets of cards, they can work in pairs to make more sets. Take photos as they build with construction materials, or paint a picture, or eat an apple.

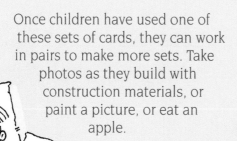

Talk about whether you can always tell which picture came first. Try these on the left.

Days of the week

Give children a strip of paper with seven spaces in a row, like this:

As each day goes by, ask them to draw or write about something special that happened that day. (If they are stuck for ideas, they could draw what they had for dinner, what they were wearing, or what the weather was like.)

Yesterday	Today	Tomorrow	
Monday	Tuesday	Wednesday	Thursd

Make a strip of card, the same length as three days, with 'Yesterday, Today, Tomorrow' written on it.

Put the week on display, and move 'Today' along to the right place each day. Add one or two more weeks to the frieze if you can, for further practice.

Seasons

Your aim when you tackle this topic (on four occasions during the year, in each season) is to help children be more observant, so that they see for themselves the differences in the weather, and in plants and trees. Try not to be misleading; it does not always snow in the winter, and it is not always sunny in the summer! Take photos in the school grounds in September, January, April and June, or get children to paint or draw what they see. Look at them all together in June, to compare the seasons.

Clocks

Go clock spotting! Ask children to sketch as many clocks as they can find, at school and at home. Put the sketches in a book or on display.

Borrow a chiming clock. Count the chimes on the 'o'clock' times.

Chalk a big clock face on the playground. Run round it clockwise.

© PHOTODISC, INC

Shape all around us

One of the most important ways in which we can help children improve their work in shape and space is to work on their observational skills. Simply bringing children's attention to things around them, including both natural and man-made shapes and patterns, and talking about what they can see, is very helpful.

Children need as wide a vocabulary as possible to be able to talk and think about shape and space. Learning even one new word can take quite a long time, particularly if the word describes a mathematical idea that is new to the child. Children need to hear the word very frequently, to say it out loud as often as possible, and to use it when describing or explaining things to you, so that you can check they have fully understood it.

Be especially careful about words that may have a completely different meaning in a different context, as this is confusing for many children. For example, a child who is used to hearing the word 'straight' in sentences like 'We're going straight home' (meaning as quickly as possible, without stopping) may initially be puzzled when asked to draw a straight line.

Model making and sketching are both valuable ways of helping children think about shape and space. When you make a model or draw something, you have to think about the most important features of the shapes you are interested in, and include them.

Dough models

Children can use dough, clay, or other modelling materials to make models of animals, people or other things around them. Ask them to think and talk about the most important feature of each shape. For example, people can tell this toy animal is a giraffe because it has a long neck. Have them look at their model from above, from the front and from the back. Does it look 'in proportion' so that, for example, its head is not too big for the size of its body?

Small lumps of Blu-Tack or similar material are useful for making tiny models.

Frames and telescopes

Help children to concentrate on looking carefully at a pattern or shape by giving them a card 'frame' to look through or lending them a 'telescope' (a cardboard tube).

A magnifying glass can also help children concentrate.

Pattern spotting

Children look for patterns and shapes around the classroom.

Ask them to draw a sketch of a pattern they have seen. Can their partner spot the pattern?

> The zigzags are on Jamie's jumper. The frogs are on our curtains.

Jigsaws

Jigsaws encourage children to think about shape, colour and position. We each have our favourite tactics for completing a jigsaw, and it helps children to think logically if an adult talks to them about how they could do the jigsaw. A jigsaw with a picture to refer to is very helpful for developing vocabulary about position.

> Can you find blue pieces, for the sky at the top?

> The flowers are all in the right-hand corner.

> Can you find the four corner pieces?

Extra Help in **Maths**
Ages 5–7 NC Level 1 Scottish Level A

Building and drawing

While some children learn new words very quickly, low-attaining children may need much more practice to remember new words and to be confident that they are using them correctly.

Model-making, playing with the things they have made, and drawing their models can be a very helpful way of providing opportunities to use mathematical vocabulary.
Of course, if a child is working on his own, he is unlikely to talk much – he needs another child or an adult to discuss things with.

Sometimes you may be surprised to find that children are uncertain about everyday words that are used to describe position. Often this is because we use the word in different ways at different times. For example, if you ask a child to 'move the counter forwards' when you are playing a board game, you want them to move it further along the track – which might actually be sideways!
Talk to children about the fact that it is sometimes confusing, but that they can always ask questions to check what people mean.

Practical work is welcome and enjoyable for many children who have difficulty with maths, especially if it uses a context that they are interested in. Low-attaining children may need more practice than most at using scissors, sticky tape and glue. Offer adult help to avoid high levels of frustration, but avoid doing too much for the child; otherwise their skills will not improve. Consolidate skills by providing another opportunity as soon as possible to repeat an activity they have enjoyed, perhaps at home.

Spot the difference

Make two models, with one difference. Can the children change just one piece to make both models the same?

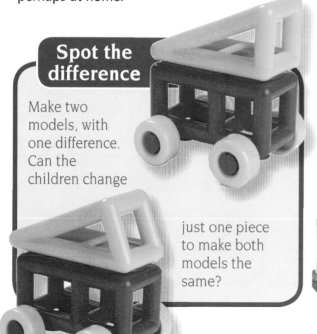

Copy me

Some low-attaining children are expert and imaginative when using plastic construction equipment such as Lego or Mobilo. It provides them with a welcome chance to show how well they can   do. Others are less confident, and will benefit from copying other people's models.

Can you make a model exactly like this one?

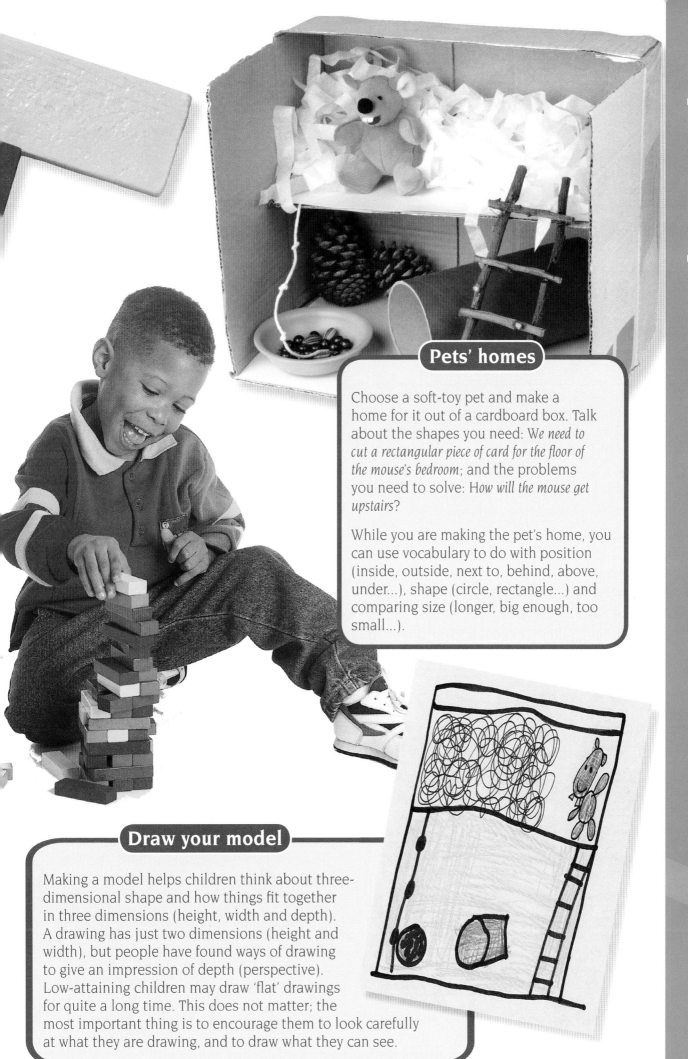

Pets' homes

Choose a soft-toy pet and make a home for it out of a cardboard box. Talk about the shapes you need: *We need to cut a rectangular piece of card for the floor of the mouse's bedroom*; and the problems you need to solve: *How will the mouse get upstairs?*

While you are making the pet's home, you can use vocabulary to do with position (inside, outside, next to, behind, above, under...), shape (circle, rectangle...) and comparing size (longer, big enough, too small...).

Draw your model

Making a model helps children think about three-dimensional shape and how things fit together in three dimensions (height, width and depth). A drawing has just two dimensions (height and width), but people have found ways of drawing to give an impression of depth (perspective). Low-attaining children may draw 'flat' drawings for quite a long time. This does not matter; the most important thing is to encourage them to look carefully at what they are drawing, and to draw what they can see.

counting

One, two, three, four, five,

Once I caught a fish alive.

Six, seven, eight, nine, ten,

Then I let it go again.

Why did you let it go?

Because it bit my finger so.

Which finger did it bite?

This little finger on my right.

© Scholastic Ltd 2004

Extra Help in **Maths**
Ages 5–7 NC Level 1 Scottish Level A

■SCHOLASTIC
PHOTOCOPIABLE

See page 17 in text.

Counting

How to make salt dough

1. You need a mug. Measure one mug of salt and two mugs of plain flour.

2. Mix the salt and flour together.

3. Add a dessertspoon of cooking oil.

4. Add some cold water, a bit at a time, and keep mixing until you have made a dough.

5. Use your dough to make small animals.

Hedgehog
Snail

6. Bake in a cool oven (140°C) for an hour or two, until they have dried hard. Then you can paint them if you want to.

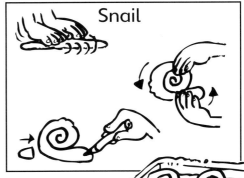

See page 19 in text.

Lorry counting cards

Print four copies on to card to make eight counting cards.

counting

Extra Help in **Maths**
Ages 5–7 NC Level 1 Scottish Level A

SCHOLASTIC
PHOTOCOPIABLE

See page 19 in text.

Elephant counting cards

Print four copies on to card to make eight counting cards.

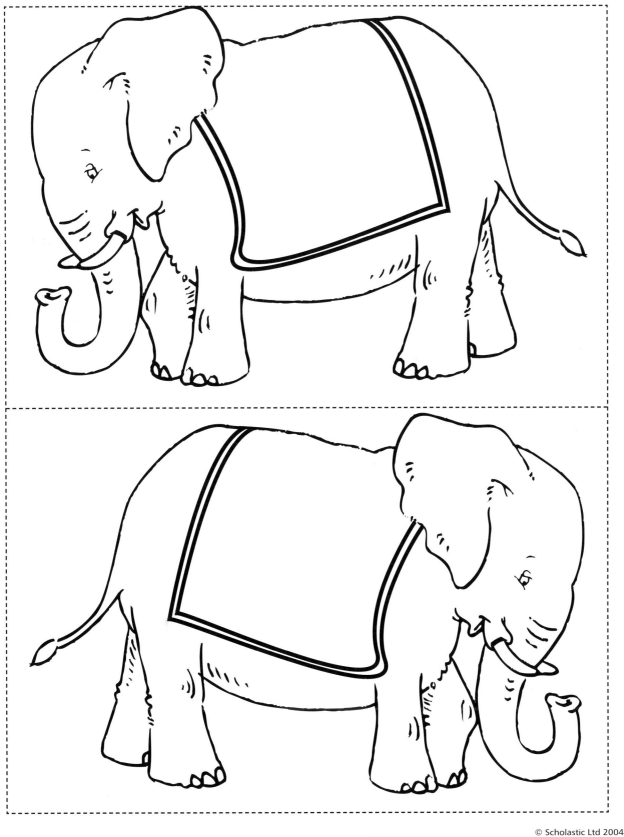

counting

See page 23 in text.

Noisy cards game

Print on to card and cut out. Paperclip the set of noisy cards together. There are two spare cards for you to make your own.

counting

Noisy Cards	Choose a number card and a sound card.  Squeak! Squeak! Squeak!	3
4	5	6
 squeak	 miaow	 beep
 hissssss		

Extra Help in **Maths**
Ages 5–7 NC Level 1 Scottish Level A

SCHOLASTIC
PHOTOCOPIABLE

See page 27 in text.

Dinosaurs

Photocopy at this size, or enlarge to A3. Make more than one copy, if necessary. Colour them, cut them out and count them. Make a poster with moveable dinosaurs.

counting

See page 29 in text.

Cut-out numbers

Photocopy this sheet on to card. Cut out each number. Stick the numbers on to a rectangle of card to make it easier to hold them still for crayon rubbing.

You can cut through the numbers to cut out the holes because these numbers are going to be stuck on to a backing card.

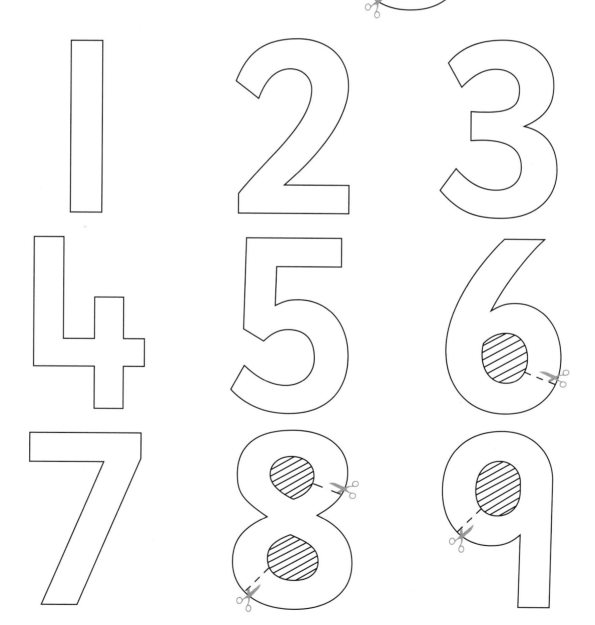

See pages 30 and 31 in text.

Name _____ Date _____

Writing numbers

Which numbers can you write neatly? **Always** start at the top of each number.

If you are left-handed, you might prefer writing your numbers slightly differently.

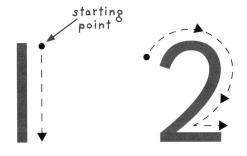

starting point

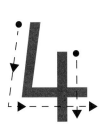

Remember: a 5 must have a straight line at the top, otherwise it might look like an 'S'.

Put numbers into small groups to practise writing them:

| 2 and 3 | 5 and 9 | 1 and 7 |

| 4 and 5 | 6, 8 and 0 |

© Scholastic Ltd 2004

Extra Help in **Maths**
Ages 5–7 NC Level 1 Scottish Level A

reading and writing numbers

See page 41 in text.

Price labels

Print one or two copies on to card and cut them out. Use them to put prices on toys in a toy shop.

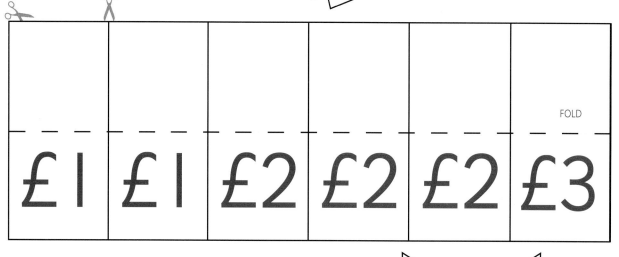

£1 | £1 | £2 | £2 | £2 | £3

FOLD

£3 | £3 | £4

SPECIAL OFFER £1

SPECIAL OFFER £2

SPECIAL OFFER £3

addition and subtraction

Extra Help in **Maths**
Ages 5–7 NC Level 1 Scottish Level A

What comes first?

Photocopy on to card and cut out. Paperclip each set together in random order.

		Know the number names in order, forwards and backwards.	Count groups of objects reliably, 0 to 10, then beyond.	Count reliably in other contexts, such as sounds and actions.	Count in twos.	Recognise numbers 0 to 10, then beyond.	Write numbers 0 to 10, then beyond.	Order numbers and position them on a number track or number line.	Give a sensible estimate of a number of objects that can be checked by counting.	Understand the operation of addition, and ...
number — Songs and rhymes	12	●	○			○				
Counting books and stories	14	●	●				●	●		
Collections	16	●	●		○	○	○			○
Counting games	18	●	●		○	●	●			○
Bags and boxes	20	○	●	○						●
Sounds and actions	22	●		●	○	●	●			
Track games	24	○		●	○	○	●	●		
Counting all around us	26	●	●		○	○	○			○
Reading numbers	28	●	●			●				
Writing numbers	30	●	●				●	●	○	
calculations — Practical problems	34	○	●				●	●		○
Using the number line	36	●	●	●	●	●	●	●		
Number facts	38	○	●				○	●		
Money	40	○	●		●		○	○		○
measures, shape and space — Length	44	○	○	○			●	●	●	
Time	46	●		●			●	●		
Shape all around us	48	○	○				○			
Building and drawing	50									

numbers and the number system

The teaching and learning objectives in this book are matched to the National Curriculum's Attainment Targets for Mathematics at Level 1:

Attainment target 1: using and applying mathematics
Pupils use mathematics as an integral part of classroom activities. They represent their work with objects or pictures and discuss it. They recognise and use a simple pattern or relationship.

Attainment target 2: number and algebra
Pupils count, order, add and subtract numbers when solving problems involving up to ten objects. They read and write the numbers involved.

Attainment target 3: shape, space and measures
When working with 2-D and 3-D shapes, pupils use everyday language to describe properties and positions. They measure and order objects using direct comparison, and order events.

Summary of teaching and learning objectives, matched to *The National Numeracy Strategy* (England), *Framework for Teaching Mathematics from Reception to Year 6*. All at Level 1 of the National Curriculum.

Separate (partition) a given number of objects into two groups.	Use knowledge that addition can be done in any order to do calculations more efficiently.	Begin to recognise that more than two numbers can be added together.	Begin to use the +, − and = signs to record calculations in a number sentence, and to recognise the use of symbols to stand for an unknown number.	Solve simple problems or puzzles in a practical context and respond to 'What could we try next?'	Explain methods and reasoning orally.	Begin to understand and use the vocabulary related to money. Sort coins and use them in role play to pay and give change.	Understand and use the vocabulary related to length. Compare lengths by direct comparison.	Measure length using uniform non-standard and standard units.	Use vocabulary related to time. Sequence familiar events. Know days of the week and seasons of the year. Read o'clock time.	Use everyday language to describe features of familiar 3-D and 2-D shapes.	Use everyday words to describe position, direction and movement.
				○	○						
				●	○						
○	○			○	○						
○	○			●	○						
○				●	●						
				●	○						
				●	●						
				●	○						
				○	○						
				●	○						
○	●	●	●	●	●						
	●	●	●	●	●						
●	○		●	●	●						
●	○	●		●	●	●					
				●	●		●	●	●	○	○
				●	○				●		●
				●	●	○	○	○		●	●
				●	●		●	●		●	●

calculations — **solving problems** — **measures, shape and space**

● main focus   ○ also useful

Summary of objectives

Summary of teaching and learning objectives, matched to *Curriculum and Assessment in Scotland, National Guidelines, Mathematics 5–14*. All at Level A.

	measures, shape and space				calculations				number								
	Building and drawing	Shape all around us	Time	Length	Money	Number facts	Using the number line	Practical problems	Writing numbers	Reading numbers	Counting all around us	Track games	Sounds and actions	Bags and boxes	Counting games	Collections	Counting books and stories 14
	50	48	46	44	40	38	36	34	30	28	26	24	22	20	18	16	
Problem solving and enquiry	●	●	●	●	●	●	●	●	●	●	●	●	●	●	●	●	●
Number, money and measurement																	
Range and type of numbers: Work with whole numbers 0 to 20.		○	○	○	●	●	●	●	●	●	●	●	●	●	●	●	●
Money: Use 1p, 2p, 5p, 10p and 20p coins to buy things.					●												
Add and subtract: Mentally for numbers 0 to 10; in applications in number, measurement and money.						●	●	●						●	○		○
Patterns and sequences: Work with simple number sequences; copy, continue and describe simple patterns.		●			○												
Measure and estimate: Measure in convenient non-standard units of length; estimate length; use and understand vocabulary of length.	●	●		●													
Time: Place events in time sequences including days and seasons; tell the time in whole hours.			●														
Shape, position and movement																	
Range of shapes: Classify shapes by simple properties; identify and name squares, rectangles, triangles and circles.	●	●															
Range of shapes (continued): Create or copy 3-D structures using building blocks or everyday objects.	●	●										○					
Position and movement: Discuss position and movement.	●	●															

● main focus   ○ also use